DISCUSSION PAPER 62

I0122930

ETHNICITY AND DEMOCRATISATION IN AFRICA
Challenges for Politics and Development

OSITA A. AGBU

NORDISKA AFRIKAINSTITUTET, UPPSALA 2011

Indexing terms:
Ethnicity
Ethnic conflicts
Interethnic relations
Democratization
Politics
Nation-building
Citizenship
Africa

Language checking: Peter Colenbrander

ISSN 1104-8417

ISBN 978-91-7106-699-2

© The author and Nordiska Afrikainstitutet 2011

Production: Byrå4

Print on demand, Lightning Source UK Ltd.

Contents

Foreword...5

Abstract...6

Introduction...7

Revisiting the Literature 8

Exploring the Linkage(s) 12

Some Theoretical Perspectives on Ethnicity 14

Emerging Issues..19

Democratisation in Post-Cold War Africa: Emerging Challenges 21

References..25

Foreword

This Discussion Paper provides a conceptual exploration of the connections between ethnicity and democratisation in post-Cold War Africa. Its point of departure is the understanding that the ethnicity-democracy nexus, though problematic, is of critical importance to an explanation of politics and development in Africa. The fundamental question raised is whether ethnicity can be reconciled with the struggles for citizenship rights and democracy in the context of the "unfinished" nation-state project in Africa. This is an issue that resonates with the debate on the larger question of whether ethnicity obstructs or advances democracy in Africa. The author, while acknowledging the widespread view that ethnicity tends to complicate issues, fuel conflict and pose serious challenges for democracy, cautions against the dismissal of ethnicity as a factor that is relevant to democratisation on the continent. In terms of the conception of ethnicity, the author draws on its manifestations in political and economic life, and warns against any "ethnic determinism" in the analysis of politics and conflicts in Africa. The paper explores both the concepts of ethnicity and democratisation in the African context, and follows this with a discussion of the linkages between both. This forms the basis for examining the emerging challenges facing ethnicity and democratisation in Africa. Of note in this regard is the observation that ethnicity is critical to understanding the politics of civil society and the struggles that underpin the nation-state project. It is also noted that in some contexts, where certain sections of a country have been marginalised, ethnic resurgence can take the form of demands for inclusion by way of democratic representation. In the concluding section, the author makes a case for the management of ethnic diversities by African states in ways that bring together ethnicity and citizenship within the framework of inclusive democratisation. This Discussion Paper will be of interest to scholars and practitioners working in the fields of African political science, development, peace and security.

Cyril Obi
Senior Researcher
The Nordic Africa Institute

Abstract

This paper revisits existing viewpoints on the nexus between ethnicity and democratisation in Africa. It seeks to explore and explain the linkages between the two concepts as key factors in shaping political developments on the continent. This overview addresses the question of whether ethnicity facilitates or obstructs democratisation in Africa in light of the resurgence of ethnic nationalism. Generally, the critical issues pertaining to ethnicity and state-society relations have assumed greater prominence in the face of the crisis of citizenship that is posing challenges to the postcolonial nation-state project in Africa. These issues also underscore the ways in which ethnicity and democratisation respond to developments within African societies as well as changes in a rapidly globalising world. The point is that the concept of ethnicity and its implications for democratisation cannot be taken for granted, and produce different outcomes in different states. Arising from the review of the various perspectives on ethnicity and democratisation, it is argued that the concept of ethnicity should be nuanced when considering its role in African democracy and development. From this perspective, the article examines the theoretical challenge ethnicity poses to the postcolonial African state project, partly as a result of its implication in political instability and conflict, and the challenges it poses for democratisation on the continent.

Introduction

There is a need for a better understanding of the problems of ethnicity and democratisation in Africa. This is partly because of the tendency to view ethnic difference as a major cause or driver of civil wars or political instability in Africa. Closely related to this is the whole question of the relationship between ethnicity and citizenship in emerging nation states, where there seems to be a contradiction between loyalty to the ethnic group and the nation state. On the surface, this appears to be a problem in many multiethnic African nation states with histories of marginalising certain ethnic groups or entire regions from the distribution of power and resources, but becomes rather complicated in cases like Somalia, where everyone is Somali, but divided along clan lines. There is also the problem of ethnic boundaries and the constructed nature of ethnicity and the reality that it is dynamic and can change or respond to different factors or interests. Thus, while it may be necessary to be wary of falling into the trap of some form of ethnic determinism when dealing with African politics and conflict, it is equally important not to dismiss ethnicity altogether, but to understand when and under what conditions it becomes relevant, and when it is not. More important is the need to develop a set of tools with which to observe the nexus between ethnicity and democratisation and explain that it is neither fixed nor inevitable but depends on history, culture, politics and economics and the character of the state in Africa.

In Africa therefore, the phenomenon of ethnicity and its dynamics need to be thoroughly understood, both at the level of conception and its manifestation in political and economic life. This paper assumes more relevance when it is considered that ethnic identity, when mobilised in the pursuit of politics, interrogates the very notion of nationhood and by extension, national citizenship in Africa, a situation that has wider implications for peace, development and security. It should be noted that the view that ethnicity works against democracy is not peculiar to Africa. It has also been observed in Eastern Europe and the former Soviet Union that a major reason for the failure of democratisation has been ethnic-based conflicts (Nzongola-Ntalaja 2001:35). The challenge is to interrogate these assumptions in the light of recent developments in Africa.

In view of the foregoing, it is important to raise some critical questions to guide the discourse. For example, what is the nature of the relationship between ethnicity and democratisation in Africa? In what ways or under what circumstances can ethnicity serve or subvert democracy? What are the major issues involved? What challenges does the resurgence of ethnic nationalism in some African countries pose for democratisation? Can ethnicity be reconciled with the struggles for citizenship rights and democracy within the "unfinished" nation-state project in Africa?

Revisiting the Literature

The literature on ethnicity and democratisation suggests that the linkages between both may be complex, given the varied interpretations that the concepts can be subjected to. According to Chazan (1992:106), ethnicity denotes the complexity of human existence and behaviour and defies simplistic definition. It signifies perceptions of common origins, historical memories, identity and common ties between people. It has its foundations in memories of past experiences and common aspirations, values, norms and expectations. Nnoli (1978:5) defines ethnicity as a social phenomenon associated with interactions among members of different ethnic groups. He further defined ethnic groups as social formations distinguished by the communal character of their boundaries, with the relevant communal factors being language, culture or both. Also, he noted that ethnicity is behavioural in form and conflictual in content and that it exists only within a political society consisting of diverse ethnic groups. In buttressing this assertion, Nnoli (1995:6) observed that ethnic-group access to state power or the lack of it is an important element in ethnic politics, especially if minority groups are denied access to power and resources based on the small(er) size of their population (even in contexts where they contribute more to national wealth), and that this is likely to lead to increased ethnic consciousness. He opined that in Africa, access to state power is important for the various ethnic groups because of the extensive intervention of the African state in the political and socioeconomic spheres.

Contributing to the discourse, Anugwom (2000:64) sees ethnicity as arising from a situation where a group of people, no matter how small, with different cultural and linguistic attributes from those of its neighbours, use this as the basis for solidarity and interaction with others. In his view, the sociocultural consciousness and solidarity of the group plays an important role in the interaction with other groups, especially in terms of competition for power and resource allocation within the nation state. Osaghae (1995:11) defines ethnicity as the employment and/or mobilisation of ethnic identity or difference to seek advantage in situations of competition, conflict or cooperation. He sees the ethnic group as one whose members share a common identity and affinity based on a common language and culture, myth of a common origin and territorial homeland, which becomes a basis for differentiation. Commenting on the issue of ethnic distinctiveness and boundaries, Barth (1969:11) had noted that categorical distinctions do not depend on the absence of mobility, contact and information, but do entail social processes of exclusion and incorporation whereby discrete categories are maintained despite changing participation and membership in the course of individual life histories. He further observed that ethnic distinctions do not depend on an absence of social interaction and acceptance, but are, quite to the contrary, often the very foundations on which embracing social systems are built.

From an anthropological point of view, Barth went on to describe an ethnic group as being based on the following: biological self-perpetuation; common cultural values realised in overt unity in cultural forms; possession of a field of communication and interaction; a membership which identifies itself and is identified by others and constitutes a category distinguishable from other categories of the same order. Shehadi (1993:105), dwelling on the same issue, noted that ethnic identity is objective to the extent that it denotes specific historical, cultural and linguistic traits that distinguish one group from the other. He, however, observed that the objective attributes are often amenable to subjective manoeuvres accentuated by some real or felt sense of deprivation and denial.

Determining what is or is not an ethnic group appears simple. However, the problem arises when one group is in competition with another, or others. In such cases, it is possible for ethnic identities to become very fluid, so fluid indeed that it is plausible to now say that ethnic-group identity may be socially constructed. This perception was aptly captured by Lemarchand (1999:2), when he observed that:

> Ethnicity is never what it seems. What looks like ancestral atavism others iden-
> tify as a typically modern phenomenon, anchored in the impact of colonial rule.
> Where neo-Marxists detect class interests parading in traditional garb, main-
> stream scholars unveil imagined communities. And what many see as the bane of
> the continent, others view as the basis of a moral social contract that carries the
> seeds of accountability and transparency.

This gives us a good idea of the conceptual complexity of what we are trying to explain. Indeed, as Lemarchand noted in the case of the Rwandan genocide in 1994, questions arise as to the meaning of ethnicity when groups that had shared the same values, customs and space for centuries suddenly descend violently on each other. Perhaps, seeking an explanation, Anderson (1983) came up with the idea of "imagined communities," as he tried to delineate the processes through which the "nation" came to be imagined, and, once imagined, modelled, adapted and transformed. In concerning himself with social change and the different forms of consciousness, he believed that beneath the decline of sacred communities, languages and lineages, a fundamental change was taking place in modes of understanding the world, which, more than anything else, made it possible to "think" the nation.

In sum, certain denominators such as the fact of common origins, common historical experiences, common aspirations and attributes like language and culture are clearly evident as features that may delineate what an ethnic group is. Also, understandable is the view that ethnic conflicts may arise in situations of competition or in situations of interaction among two or more ethnic groups. In other words, perceived threats to the viability of the group's culture or interests may be taken as threats to individual members and may provoke a violent reaction (Wippman 1998:4). But then the question arises, are these interests really communal or individualistic? Deciphering the web between individual interests and group interests is another very problematic aspect of ethnic studies, which invariably has implications for the various democratisation processes occurring in Africa.

On the other hand, the literature on democratisation, which basically refers to the process of liberalising state-society relations, indicates that democratisation, though a widespread concept, is also a contested one. For example, Olowu et al. (1995) define democratisation as the movement from the dominance of state-society relations by one institution (usually the executive branch) to a polycentric structured society. Nwokedi (1995:17) was of the view that democratisation is the process of a shift away from non-democratic forms of government towards democracy and that it may equally refer to the expansion of democratic space or performance within a democratic polity. Nwabueze (1993) adopted a wider view of democratisation as a concept synonymous with multipartyism but also including other conditions such as a virile civil society; a democratic society; a just society; a free society; equal treatment of all citizens by the state; and an ordered and stable society infused with the spirit of liberty, democracy, justice and equality. In his contribution, Horowitz (1994) pointed out that although democratisation is a worldwide phenomenon, it is neither universal nor uniform in places where it exists. He also observed that democracy is basically about inclusion and exclusion, about access to power, about the privileges that go with inclusion and the penalties that accompany exclusion. While the spirit of competition may be seen as healthy for democracy, anchoring this competition on ethnicity or ethnic factors may be counterproductive to the movement towards democratisation and democracy, and that ethnic conflict may negate the developmental function of democracy (Anugwom 2000:67).

However, there is another perspective that is critical of the dominant paradigm of liberal Western democracy, noting that it is of limited relevance to the interests and aspirations of the majority of Africans (Ake 1993, 2000; Lumumba-Kasongo 2005). In this view, Western democracy, with its emphasis on procedures and multiparty elections, hardly focuses on the content and context of democracy, reducing it to an intra-class competition for power (Ninsin 2006:3). Arguing along these lines, Ake (1993) concludes that "ruling elites perceive of democracy as more a means than an end, a strategy for power, while for the masses it is a struggle for socio-economic emancipation and democratic inclusion." In this regard, the view that liberal democracy in Africa is a limited democratic opening that does permit some form of participation and accountability (via periodic elections) but does not go far enough to empower the majority of African people. Rather, it enables the elite (minority) to dominate political and economic power. In this regard, ethnicity's impact on politics and democratisation may depend on two issues: how it is susceptible to manipulation by the dominant elite, and the ways in which identity may become a platform for excluded groups to organise and struggle for group interests.

More recent literature on ethnicity has connected the wider discourse of identity-based conflicts as manifestations of the crisis of citizenship in Africa. Therefore, "the concept of national citizenship, of equal rights, benefits and duties for all citizens has been attenuated or bifurcated, with the state sunk in a cesspool of inter-group struggles and conflicts over the distribution of public goods" (Adejumobi 2005:20). What this suggests also is that the postcolonial state is implicated in the denial of citizenship rights to those considered outsiders, non-citizens or lesser citizens. It also explains why in some countries, ethnicity has become a mobilising tool for confronting the legitimacy of the state. This can be gleaned from the activities of the New Forces (based in northern Côte d'Ivoire) that rebelled against the Ivorian state in the early part of the first decade of the 21st century (Yere 2007), the agitation of the Odu'a People's Congress protesting the marginalisation of the Yoruba in the 1990s in Nigeria, the Movement for the Sovereign State of Biafra (MASSOB) in South East Nigeria (Omeje 2005; Metumara 2010; Adekson 2004), and the insurgency against the Nigerian federal government by the Movement for the Emancipation of the Niger Delta (MEND) (Ukoha 2007; Okonta 2007).

From the foregoing, it is clear that ethnicity is relevant to the struggle for democracy in Africa. It plays a crucial role in the struggle to determine who will eventually be included or excluded from access to state resources, power and political representation (Adejumobi 2005). In many African countries where multiparty democracy has been formally institutionalised and where there is a history of complaints of ethnic domination/exclusion, there is always the risk that dominant ethnic elites may resort to majoritarian rule in the context of zero-sum politics. When this happens, the result is often post-election conflicts, with excluded groups inevitably protesting the outcomes of elections that they perceive as being skewed against them in the first place.

In some cases, efforts at political engineering aimed at diffusing the ethnic tensions that accompany multiparty elections in Africa have taken the form of inclusive power-sharing arrangements or governments of national unity that seek to accommodate otherwise excluded elites. Thus, if not properly managed, ethnicity in the context of democratisation could contribute to intractable conflicts. Therefore, an exploration of the linkages between ethnicity and democratisation is germane to the analysis of socio-political development in Africa.

Exploring the Linkage(s)

There is little doubt that in the main, ethnicity and democratisation are interconnected in the context of African development. We cannot address democracy without considering the influence of ethnicity on political behaviour, including voting patterns and elite politics, while ethnicity only becomes relevant as a result of the politicisation of ethnic identity in the struggle for power or political competition. It is also possible to argue that the situation sometimes is almost akin to an antithesis as the two concepts appear to be in contention in the nation-building project in Africa. Attempts to suppress ethnicity in the first decade of independence in many African countries did not quite succeed. Rather, what is noticeable is that in the face of the crisis of citizenship and the nation-state project in many African states, and increased globalisation, ethnicity has resurged, posing challenges for democratisation.

As explicated in the seminal scholarship of Bangura in his work on identities, when the modern states were created by European powers in Africa, the mono-ethnic idea of the nation state was foisted upon diverse societies, which in many cases had large numbers of ethnic groups. Thus, post-Second World War nationalism in Africa often took place within the colonial states created by the European imperial powers. The common view among the then nationalists was that only the state could build a new, homogenous and united community, which meant subordinating diverse ethnic groups to a single national logic. This in turn proved to be problematic in the face of historically constructed inequalities and disparities. In the process, nations created by postcolonial states ended up alienating or marginalising some ethnic groups, particularly when the nation-state project was led by an authoritarian/single party or military regime. Thus the idea of the multiethnic nation state in Africa was problematic right from its inception and fed into interethnic tensions during the period of economic crisis and pressures for democracy in the 1980s.

Generally, democracy in its populist form tries to eliminate ethnic conflict by pursuing the policy of "national self-determination" on the one hand, and dealing with individual rights often at the expense of group rights or identities. In this regard, the expectation is that patriotism would create a transcendent territorial community. A new people (nation) will be created in the process of state-building, complemented by emerging anti-elite class interests of either the working people or the middle class (Glickman 1995:5). Perhaps it was because of this mode of thinking in the social sciences, especially after the Second World War, that little attention was paid to the "ethnic question" (Stavenhagen, 1990:6). It is only since the 1980s that scholars in Africa have refocused attention on the study of *ethnie* and its related aspects of ethnic identity, interethnic relations and ethnic conflicts.

Generally, the relationship between ethnicity and democratisation appears to be that of contradictions on the one hand, and complementarity on the other. As observed by Horowitz (1994:6), given the dilemma of multiparty politics, it is reasonable to maintain that in ethnically divided societies majority rule will not be a solution but a problem, because it permits the domination of one group, which is in the majority, over the others. This creates some sort of fear among the dominated groups, which could lead to conflict. Now this is just one side of the coin: the other is that the genuine incorporation of ethnicity or the inclusion of ethnic concerns may contribute to stability in the system, or to the development of democracy. In this case, ethnicity performs legitimate political functions and is important in deeply divided societies. It could perform this role when ethnic differences are recognised and an acceptable formula worked out among the various groups in the society for including ethnic concerns in the design of the democratic process.

Anugwom (2000) notes that some level of ethnic conflict or rivalry should be expected in ethnically plural societies and that, indeed, when these conflicts are non-violent they may be regarded as a contributory factor to social development. On the other hand, when these conflicts are violent and threaten democratic transitions, as in the case of Nigeria, or underpin mass violence, as in Rwanda, Burundi and the Democratic Republic of Congo (DRC), ethnicity becomes a contributory factor in social disintegration and crisis (Anugwom 2000:69).

The salience of the centrifugal forces pulling in the opposite direction to that of the forces of democratisation is quite insightful and has serious implications for the democratisation process in Africa (Ake 1992). Note, for instance, the difficulties of democratisation in Nigeria, Kenya, the DRC and Ghana. In fact, respected authorities in this field like Nnoli (1995:24) identified certain intervening variables that serve as obstacles to democracy in the context of ethnic pluralities. These include the extent of the role of the state in the society, the class character of the national leadership and the history of interethnic relations, especially the critical moments of violence or the serious threat of it.

Today, with political liberalisation and the adoption of liberal democratic constitutions in many African countries, two important stages in the process of democratisation have been identified: issues that have been suppressed are restating their claims on the state while groups that have been oppressed are openly reasserting their identities. As Akwetey (1996:104), notes, this reassertion of identities and restating of claims usually manifest themselves, depending on the prevailing social and political conditions, either as ethno-political protests or rebellion. In addition, the declining capacity of many postcolonial African states to ensure personal and economic security is another major reason for the exacerbation of ethnic conflicts, as the different groups struggle with each other for access to resources and power. Though the struggles for democracy have been largely defined in terms of the quest for the expansion of political space, human rights, civil liberties and economic, social and cultural rights, the reality is that ethnically instigated conflicts are embedded in the ongoing political struggles.

Ethnicity may pose obstacles at the threshold of democratisation and even after the threshold is crossed (Horowitz 1994:37). Therefore, it can be argued that under certain circumstances a strong and conflictual link exists between democratisation as a process of governance and ethnicity. The challenge for us is to determine the organising framework around which democratic principles can be guaranteed on the one hand, while also responding to and respecting group interests in ethnically diverse societies.

Some Theoretical Perspectives on Ethnicity

There are several perspectives in the study of ethnicity and ethnic conflicts, some major, others highly compartmentalised. Lake and Rothchild (1996) proffer three broad approaches to the study of ethnicity and ethnic conflict. These are the primordialist, instrumentalist and constructivist approaches. They arrived at these categorisations following a critical analysis of the perspectives of the different scholars and policy-makers who participated in the University of California-based Institute on Global Conflict and Cooperation (IGCC) Project on the International Spread and Management of Ethnic Conflicts.

According to the authors, the primordialist approach takes ethnicity as a fixed characteristic of individuals and communities (Kaplan 1993; Connor 1994). Whether rooted in inherited biological attributes or centuries of past practice now beyond the ability of individuals or groups to alter, one is invariably and always a Serb, a Zulu, a Swede or a Chechen. In this view, ethnic divisions and tensions are "natural." Although recognising that ethnic warfare is not a constant state of affairs, primordialists see conflicts as flowing from ethnic differences and, therefore, not necessarily in need of explanation. The most frequent criticism of the primordialist approach is its assumption of fixed identities and its failure to account for variations in the level of conflict over time and place. The approach does not seem capable of explaining the emergence of new and transformed identities, or to account for the long periods when ethnicity is not conflictual.

The instrumentalist approach presents ethnicity as a tool used by individuals, groups or elites to attain some larger, typically material end (Brass 1985; Rothchild 1986). In this view, ethnicity has little independent standing outside the political process in which collective ends are sought. Therefore, ethnicity is primarily a label or set of symbolic ties used for political advantage, just like interest group membership or political party affiliation. A major criticism of this approach is that ethnicity is embedded within and controlled by the larger society: hence, it is not something that can be decided upon by individuals at will. In the alternative, critics argue that ethnicities are inherently social in nature and can only be understood within a relational framework (Esman, 1994:13).

In line with this thinking, an emerging scholarly consensus can be found in the constructivist approach, which seeks to provide the relational framework by emphasising the social origins and nature of ethnicity (Anderson 1983; Brubaker 1995). In the constructivist view, ethnicity is not an individual attribute, but a social phenomenon. A person's identity remains beyond the choice or control of that individual. Rather it is constructed from complex webs of social interactions. The Yugoslav case as an example is quite apt and revealing. Till the late 1980s, a Yugoslav identity had evolved from the cosmopolitanism of the urban areas and the incentives given by the federal government, but as the state disintegrated, this identity was broken as individuals quickly returned to their more particularistic roots as being Serb, Croatian or Bosnian. As with instrumentalists, constructivists do not see ethnicity as inherently conflictual. Rather, conflict is caused by certain pathological factors in the social system, which individuals do not control. In this view, it is the social system that breeds violent conflict, not individuals, and it is the socially constructed nature of ethnicity that can cause conflicts. It is important to note that constructivists' accounts of ethnic conflicts are generalisable, but only to other conflicts that are also based on socially constructed groups and cleavages. These include clan, religious, regionalist or nationalist groupings but exclude class and other material interest-based conflicts that are more likely founded on individual attributes (Lake and Rothchild 1996).

However, methodologically important for us is that whether ethnicity is socially constructed or the rational, purposive choice made by individuals and groups, the basic theoretical and research challenge is to be able to identify those social systems or conditions most prone to violence. This knowledge can then enable the search for appropriate measures to ensure that violence does not arise or recur.

Below is a table that presents a bird's-eye view of the various perspectives on ethnicity. This table does not lay claim to being exhaustive, but only serves as a succinct account of the categorisations and associated assumptions and theories.

The table is self-explanatory and shows the variants that have been identified from the three major categories. Of these, the modernisation theory (Deutsch 1953; Morisson and Stevenson 1972; Gurr 1994) and the Marxist perspective (Nnoli 1978, 1998; Hameso 1997) have generated the greater number of polemics and discourse over the years. Equally important has been the colonial theory (Nnoli 1978; Otite 1990), while increasingly visible are the aggression theory (Dougherty and Pfaltzgraff Jr. 1996; Elingsen 2000) and the counter-hegemonic theory (Obi 2001).

Theoretical Perspectives to Ethnicity

Major Approaches	Basic Assumptions	Theories		
Primordialist	– Ethnicity as a fixed characteristic – Ethnic divisions and tensions "natural" – Conflicts emanate from ethnic differences – Ethnic identity important – Inherently conflictual	Ethnic Identity Theory	Frustration-Aggression Theory	Primordial Loyalties Theory
Instrumentalist	– Ethnicity as a tool used by individuals and groups – Ethnicity thrives within the political process – Ethnicity part and parcel of similar political affiliations – Not inherently conflictual	Colonial Theory	Marxist/ Dependency Perspective	Modernisation Theory
Constructivist	– Ethnicities are of a social nature – Ethnicity to be understood within a "relational framework" – Ethnicity constructed from webs of social interactions – Not an individual attribute but a social phenomenon Not inherently conflictual	Social Interactionist Perspective	Counter-Hegemonic Theory	Structural-Models perspective

* This table was derived from the literature survey by author.

Let us briefly look at the foregoing theoretical perspectives. The modernisation theory as it relates to ethnicity basically posits that as far as citizens agree to transfer their allegiances and affiliation away from parochial identities to the larger society, there will be a tendency for greater political and economic integration and interaction among people (Deutsch 1953). It regards the state as the confluence of individual wills and places it above the particular interests of any specific group. During the better part of the Cold War, most scholars believed that modernisation would lead to decline in ethnic conflagration, to be replaced by loyalties to the larger societies. To many of the nationalists and African leaders who received the mantle of leadership after independence, the nation-state project was very attractive as it promised not only internal order, but also development and the ability to contain the varied interests of the multifarious ethnic groupings. This would have been possible if the post-independence state was able to transcend traditional group loyalties in favour of an abstract sense of community (Nnoli 1995).

The Marxist perspective, on the other hand, relates the ethnic problem to the dynamics of class struggle. Drawing heavily on Marx's analysis of Asiatic or "prehistoric modes of production," ethnic awareness is seen as "false consciousness," which contrasts with "true" class consciousness. From this perspective, ethnicity in Africa is perceived as a false consciousness of identity often foisted on working people by the dominant class, first to mask the reality that they are being exploited, and second to prevent them from forming a class alliance with other similarly exploited classes from other ethnic groups to overthrow the dominant class. Marxist analysis gives primacy to class consciousness over ethnic consciousness, and in some cases sees the latter as a reactionary form of consciousness that should either be ignored or neutralised. In more recent applications of Marxist theory to ethnicity in Africa, ethnicity is treated as something used by the dominant elite to divide the people, or mobilise them along ethnic lines to pursue what is in reality the agenda of the political elite.

However, as Hameso (1997:14) observed, logic dictates that if ethnic consciousness and in effect ethnicity is false, as argued from this perspective, it would be less worthy of study and, indeed, should have disappeared as a phenomenon. But this has not been the case. In other words, it should not have been as resilient as it has been. The resilience and indeed resurgence of ethnicity in Africa suggests that the earlier conclusions of Marxist analysis on ethnicity need to be further interrogated.

For its part, the colonial theory simply amplifies the role of colonial administration in Africa in fostering ethnic and communal identity consciousness (Nnoli 1978, 1989; Otite 1990). Here, colonial racism served as an instrument in the colonialists' quest to control Africa's resources. In the process, however, colonial racism, which excluded Africans from power and resources, fuelled interethnic competition for access to scarce resources and gave rise to belligerent ethnic consciousness when the colonial authorities decided to grant limited concessions to the colonised people. According to Nnoli (1978:7), at times the historical and competitive aspects of this consciousness became linked. Contemporary competition may create a common consciousness among previously and historically hostile and warring sections of the same ethnic group. To understand ethnicity, therefore, it is important to know when and how the common consciousness was brought about.

The frustration-aggression theory posits that relative deprivation may give rise to frustration and this serves as a fulcrum for the mobilisation of groups, which may result in heightened consciousness and conflict (Ellingsen 2000:230). It assumes that aggression is always a consequence of frustration and that frustration often leads to aggression. It also assumes that frustration-aggression patterns are culture-bound: that is, that aggressive impulses and group/individual targets are shaped by different or various cultural systems. Therefore, the onus lies with the social system to determine means and ways of managing and locating an outlet for frustration and consequently aggression.

Succinctly, the counter-hegemonic theory, which possesses strong explanatory powers, seeks to deconstruct the currently centralised, authoritarian and crisis-ridden nation-state project in Africa as observed by Obi (2001:13). It maintains that the resurgence of ethnicity can be defined within the power relations corresponding to the nature of the reinvigorated drive by global neoliberal forces to further integrate many developing countries into the international capitalist system. The partnership between the multinationals and the national elite in countries endowed with mineral resources and the political and adverse environmental consequences of this invariably give rise to some opposition. In this opposition, ethnic identity is thus transformed into a mobilising element not only for contesting access to state power within a context of competing and conflicting ethnicity, but also as a modality for organising social forces to resist alienation, extraction and exclusion by the hegemonic coalition of the ethnic elite.

On the other hand, the structural models perspective relates to the contrast between ranked and unranked systems of ethnic stratification, a distinction that rests upon the coincidence or non-coincidence of social class and ethnic origins. According to Horowitz (1985:22), where the two coincide, it is possible to have ranked ethnic groups. But where groups are cross-class, then what you have will be unranked groups. These models, therefore, suggest that the frequency, intensity and forms of conflict vary depending on whether interethnic relations are characterised as ranked or unranked.

As an alternative to the modernisation and mobilisational perspectives, it has been argued, and correctly too, that ethnicity is an inherent aspect of social change in all culturally heterogeneous societies, and it is not possible to make ethnicity disappear. The stability of societies is not threatened by ethnicity *per se*, but by the failure of the state to explicitly recognise and mediate competing ethnic interests. This mediation and accommodation of competing interests could be achieved through some sort of political arrangement that equitably addresses diverse ethnic interests in terms of political representation, citizenship rights and access to power and national resources.

On the other hand, there is a widely held view that the emergence and sustenance of democracy and democratisation cannot be explained by any single factor (Vanhanen 1997). Indeed, it has been difficult for researchers on this subject to agree on the most appropriate theoretical explanation of democratisation. However, scholars like Lerner (1968) and Lipset (1959, 1960) connect democratisation to economic growth and modernisation and this appears to be the most influential approach in the field. Many scholars believe that certain preconditions are necessary for democratisation. These include the following – a fairly high level of economic growth, a strong middle class, a tradition of tolerance and respect for the individual, the presence of independent social groups and institutions, a market-oriented economy and the existence of elites willing to give up power (Sancton 1987). Other researchers have also emphasised that democratisation is connected to different causal factors, including historical factors, social structures and conditions, economic development, external factors, political culture and political leadership (Dahl 1971; Diamond et al. 1988).

Vanhanen (1997) postulates an evolutionary theory in which he argues that we can find an explanation for democratisation from the distribution of various resources used as sources of power. This theory invariably appears to belong to the instrumentalist conception of competition. With the emphasis on resources, power and their distribution, the possible link with politicised ethnicity rears its head once more. Therefore, there is this intricate linkage between ethnicity and democratisation at the conceptual level that has to do with how individuals and groups relate to each other and the state in the context of power relations. Whether this relationship ensures stability or is perpetually prone to conflict in a given instance depends on the nature of the society and the mechanisms put in place for the maintenance of peace and stability. The assumption, however, is that when societies are open and governance is based on transparency, accountability and free choice (between equal competitors based on fair rules), democracy tends to promote stability and non-violent resolution of conflicts.

Emerging Issues

A critical issue in the linkage between ethnicity and democracy is the transformation of civil society in many African countries. Ethnicity becomes more relevant when we seek to analyse the role of civil society in democratisation. The question that flows from this is how and to what extent does ethnicity shape civil society or its politics? What does this mean in terms of struggles by pro-democracy groups within civil society that seek to push the state to introduce democratic reforms? Is ethnicity one of the tools that dominant elites within the state can use to divide civil society and, by extension, provoke conflict?

Ethnicity often finds expression in terms of relations of power between those considered part of a group or "one of us" and those considered other or "one of them." These relations and dynamics between insiders and outsiders with respect to inclusion in or exclusion from power and access to resources are also tied to historically defined forms of class relations and positions relative to state power. It should always be considered that the relationship between ethnicity and democracy is constantly shaped by the dynamics of the relations between and interaction of the social forces within the state. With the reconfiguration of state power in the face of changes attendant on globalisation, and the declining hegemony of the centralised state in Africa (and the increased legitimation of multiparty democracy), there is growing pressure for decentralisation in various countries (Salih and Markakis 1998). This is an emerging development that cannot be "ethnic-blind" or neutral. The challenge, therefore, is one of democratising through the devolution of power to lower tiers of governance, but taking the dynamics of ethnic identities, their various manifestations and competing interests into consideration.

As noted earlier, Africa faces the reality of the existence of diverse ethnic groups initially forced into colonially defined borders as colonial states. The decision to keep these boundaries in the postcolonial era has meant that ethnic diversity and ethnicity have remained a major issue in the nation-state project in Africa. A troubling dimension to this is the nature of competing ethnicities in the context of diminishing resources and increasing urbanisation in Africa. Again, the resurgence of ethnic identity politics could emanate from perceptions by certain ethnic communities that they were under threat or being marginalised, or have lost out in their dealings with the state. Such perceptions could also be the result of perceptions of having lost out to more powerful neighbours and rivals in the competition for access to power and resources. Examples of such perceptions of marginalisation underlie the insurgency of ethnic minority militias in Nigeria's oil-rich Niger Delta (Okonta 2007), and to some extent account for the crisis in Darfur as well as the decision of South Sudan to vote for independence after decades of war against the Khartoum government.

Experiences from the attempts at democratisation in Africa show that the opening up of democratic space for the growth of the civil society also sometimes opens up society to ethnic resurgence, more often than not in the form of demands for "democracy dividends" from the party in power. Where the government is seen as favouring one ethnic group at the expense of others, or as being unable or unwilling to acquiesce in the demands for inclusion and equity, interethnic tensions often result, and in extreme cases violent conflict. Therefore, from a political and historical perspective, centralisation, rather than transcending ethnic divisions and strengthening a homogeneous nation-state project, has dialectically fuelled ethnic resurgence in the wake of economic crisis and the non-resolution of citizenship rights.

So far, the fragile postcolonial African state appears to be incapable of responding adequately to challenges that ethnic difference and interethnic power relations pose for the national democratic project. Responses have, therefore, ranged from political arrangements based on ethnic federalism, as in Ethiopia, to the power-sharing whereby the distribution of key political posts is based on geopolitical representation and spread, as is the case in Nigeria, or governments of national unity that include the opposition, as in the case of Kenya.

This section would be incomplete without some reflection on positive aspects of ethnicity (Osaghae 1995). It could, for instance, serve as an umbrella for mobilising resources and support for community development and also as a safety net for indigent members of ethnic groups in the highly competitive urban centres of Africa. However, there is always the threat that ethnicity can be used by desperate elites seeking power by any means or that their protesting their exclusion from power can sow seeds of discord in the polity. Either way, it should be noted that the relationship between ethnicity and democracy is mediated by the state. In some cases, the state becomes a site or target for ethnic conflict. Thus, the nature of the state is critical in influencing the outcome of this linkage, either in positive or negative terms. The relationship also implies that the state and its institutions have an important role to play in addressing the challenges that ethnicity may pose for the national democratic project.

Democratisation in Post-Cold War Africa: Emerging Challenges

Two major paths have been chosen for the transition to multiparty democracy and democratisation in Africa. The first was direct recourse to constitutional change of power through the ballot box in nationally organised elections, while the second was through the mechanism of the sovereign national conferences in the 1990s. This notwithstanding, ethnicity was a factor in political transitions, be it in the Anglophone, Lusophone or Francophone countries. However, careful observation of the democratisation processes showed that conflict was caused not by the diversity of peoples, but rather by the way these diversities were constructed and managed and how they related to a particular structure of power. In cases where managing diversities appeared to deepen existing cleavages or reproduce relations of domination by one group of the other, the potential that democratic opening would raise expectations of change and result in ethnic tensions when such expectations were not fulfilled was always a possibility. Such tensions have attended post-election crises in many African countries, most recently Kenya, Guinea and Nigeria. The challenge, therefore, is to find a way of democratically balancing the demands and expectations of diverse groups and building consensus through an equitable and inclusive bargaining process.

Another emerging issue deserving close attention is the relationship between ethnicity and citizenship, as the latter constitutes a key building block in democratisation and nation-building (Adejumobi 2005). It is possible to argue that a lot of the pre- and post-election conflicts in Africa are closely related to the crisis of citizenship in multiethnic societies. An example of this problem is Côte d'Ivoire, where ethnic groups organised in terms of the north and south have been divided over the issue of Ivorian citizenship since the death of the country's patriarch or founding president, Houphouët-Boigny, in 1993. Based on the concept of Ivorité or "true Ivoriness," political elites from the south have sought to exclude their northern counterparts from power, while members of the northern elite, with the backing of some neighbouring countries, have insisted on their rights as Ivorian citizens (Yere 2007:50–8). These differences eventually culminated in civil war between 2002 and 2007, ending with the signing of a power-sharing arrangement between President Laurent Gbagbo and Guillaume Soro of the New Forces (in control of the north), who took the position of prime minister. In spite of this, the non-resolution of the divisions over contested citizenship reared its head in the November 2010 presidential elections in which both Gbagbo and Allasane Quattara claimed victory, leading to the resumption of hostilities early in 2011 and the eventual defeat of Gbagbo's loyalists and Quattara's assumption of office with support of forces sympathetic to his cause and sections of the international community.

What the foregoing case shows is the issue of citizenship posing a major challenge to the ethnicity-democracy nexus. Political thinkers and politicians need to carefully address several issues: the relationship between ethnic identity and national citizenship, negotiating and reaching an equitable basis for the equal political representation of diverse ethnic groups and establishing a minimum baseline for citizens' access to basic services, welfare and resources and compensating hitherto marginalised groups within affirmative action policies and power-sharing arrangements.

The postcolonial state in Africa as well as regional organisations should as a matter of urgency engage with ethnicity in terms of its relationship to democratic governance, accountability, economic distribution, political stability and security. This will involve engaging with various social forces within civil society, and being able to forge futures in which the basic rights and interests of different ethnic groups are safeguarded within the framework of the nation state and regional organisations in the face increased globalisation and transborder movements.

For Africa to curb the propensity of political elites to exploit ethnicity, which often leads to ethnic conflicts and violence, the state should of necessity avoid policies that fuel or exacerbate marginalisation or exclusion of some groups, including ethnic/religious minorities. Given the fact that the public sector is still the major employer of salaried and wage labour and the distributor of state resources, it is imperative that some sort of power-sharing is designed through consultation to reassure eventual losers in the political process (elections) that they still have some say in political governance and would stand a good chance at competing for power on the basis of a level playing field and fair rules in the future. This also means that the state itself must undergo some transformation to make it more democratic and less of a captive to vested interests that will limit its capacity to effectively mediate competing demands and interests.

A major contributory factor to the crisis of nation-statism in Africa is the economic factor. Apart from the fact that most African countries have remained stuck in the role of primary product exporters, which makes them very vulnerable to global economic crises, the real challenge is that in most cases the economies of these countries remain extraverted and dominated by foreign businesses and a small local elite. The structural problems that flow from the nature of Africa's integration into the global economy include the susceptibility of national economies to global crises, weak forward and backward linkages between the primary product and other sectors of national economies and high levels of unemployment and poverty compounded by weak infrastructure and inadequate basic services (often concentrated in urban areas).

As a result, large sections of the populace are alienated from the formal economy and excluded from the distribution of economic benefits, which in most cases remain concentrated in the hands of a small elite with links to state and economic power. This situation of economic "disempowerment" of the majority of Africans invariably contributes to the resurgence of ethnicity as people seek alternative spaces of social protection and survival outside a state they consider as either too distant or irrelevant to their everyday survival or future aspirations. This "retreat" from the national state has in some cases led to a "return" to ethnic groupings as an organisational base from which to challenge the legitimacy of the postcolonial state, struggle to ensure that it responds to certain interests and grievances or to organise to capture it. Such contestations tend to pose challenges for democratic transitions as they work against the level playing field that is so important to the orderly functioning of the democratic process. Therefore, a lot of attention needs to be directed at economic transformation and equitable redistribution of resources in African countries as a way of addressing some of the challenges that ethnicity may pose for democracy.

Ironically, most writing on the ethnicity-democratisation nexus does not focus enough on the external factor, beyond the fact of the politicisation of ethnic identities during colonial rule. What is often not discussed is the way in which the inequalities, stereotypes and divisions sown by colonialists have survived, evolved or been reproduced in the postcolonial period mainly by political elites seeking power. The second point relates to how some sections of the African diasporas use ethnicity in keeping "national conversations" alive in the diaspora and participating in politics in their home countries. This is a resource or constituency that has not been systematically studied in terms of its impact on democratisation in Africa. Thirdly, what is the role of the international community in terms of its engagement with African elites in the context of democracy-promotion and conflict-resolution? Two issues are relevant in this regard: sensitivity/non-sensitivity to the ethnicity-democratisation nexus, and a tendency by certain international actors to be sympathetic towards certain forms of ethnic/religious identity in pursuit of their interests. This is an issue that needs to be further investigated.

It appears it is only now that Africa is facing developmental and citizenship crises that some effort is being made to explore its own inherited histories and cultures. Increasingly, scholars are looking for alternative philosophical and cultural paradigms to address the emerging challenges facing the continent. The way forward in addressing the challenges ethnicity poses for democracy and development in Africa lies in a combination of in-depth historically informed and empirically based case studies, an analysis of the role of Africa's political leadership and elites and their interests in the democratisation processes currently occurring in Africa and unlocking the ways in which ethnicity can be fully transformed into a democratic and developmental factor.

References

Adebanwi, Wale, 2007, "The carpenter's revolt: Youth, violence and the reinvention of culture in Nigeria", *Journal of Modern African Studies* 43, 3.

Adejumobi, Said, 2005, "Identity, Citizenship and Conflict: The African Experience," in Fawole, Alade W. and Charles Ukeje (eds), *The Crisis of the State and Regionalism in West Africa: Identity, Citizenship and Conflict*. Dakar: CODESRIA.

Adekson, Adedayo, 2004, *The civil society problematique: Deconstructing civility and southern Nigeria's ethnic nationalism*. London and New York: Routledge.

Agbu, Osita, 2004, "Re-inventing Federalism in Post-Transition Nigeria: Problems and Prospects, *Africa Development* XXIX, 2.

Ake, Claude, 1992, *The New World Order: A view from the South*. Lagos: Malthouse.

—, 1993, "The unique case of African democracy". *International Affairs* 96, 2.

—, 1996, *Democracy and Development in Africa*. Washington DC: Brookings Institution.

—, 2000, *The Feasibility of Democracy in Africa*. Dakar: CODESRIA.

Akwetey, Emmanuel, 1996, "Violent Ethno-Political conflicts and the Democratic challenge", in Olukoshi, Adebayo and Liisa Laakso (eds), *Challenges to the Nation-State in Africa*. Uppsala: Nordic Africa Institute.

Anderson, Benedict, 1983, *Imagined Communities: Reflections on the Origin and Spread of Nationalism*. London: Verso.

Anugwom, E. Edlyne, 2000, "Ethnic Conflict and Democracy in Nigeria: The Marginalisation Question", *Journal of Social Development in Africa* 15, 1.

Barth, Fredrick, 1969), *Ethnic Groups and Boundaries*. Oslo: Pensuntjeneste.

Brass, Paul (ed.), 1985, *Ethnic Groups and the State*. London: CroomHelm.

Chazan, Naomi, 1992, *Politics and Society in contemporary Africa*, 2nd edition. Boulder CO: Lynne Rienner.

Connor, Walker, 1994, *Ethno-nationalism: The Quest for understanding*. Princeton: Princeton University Press.

Dahl, Robert, 1971, *Polyarchy: Participation and Opposition*. New Haven: Yale University Press.

Deutsch, Karl, 1953, *Nationalism and Social Communication: An inquiry into the Foundations of Nationality*. Cambridge MA: Harvard University Press.

Diamond, Larry et al., 1988, *Democracy in Developing Countries*, 3 vols. Boulder CO: Lynne Rienner.

Dougherty, James and Robert Pfaltzgraff Jr., 1996, *Contending Theories of International Relations: A Comprehensive Survey*, 4th edition. New York: Longman.

Elington, T., 2000, "Colour Community or Ethnic Witches Brew", *Journal of conflict Resolution* 44, 2.

Glickman, Harry, 1995, *Ethnic conflict and Democratisation in Africa*. Atlanta: African Studies Association Press.

Gurr, Robert Ted, 1994, *Minorities at Risk: A Global view of Ethno-political conflicts.* Washington DC: United States Institute of Peace Press.

Hameso, Seyoum, 1997, *Ethnicity in Africa: Towards a positive approach.* London: TSC Publications.

Horowitz, L. Donald, 1985, *Ethnic Groups in Conflict.* Berkeley CA: University of California Press.

—, 1994, "Democratisation in Divided Societies", in Diamond, Larry and Marc F. Plattner (eds), *Nationalism, Ethnic conflict and Democratisation.* Baltimore: Johns Hopkins University Press.

Kaplan, Robert, 1993, *Balkan conflicts: A Journey through History.* New York: St. Martin's Press.

Lake, David and Donald Rothchild, 1996, *Ethnic fears and Global Engagement: The International Spread and Management of Global Conflicts.* IGCC Conference on the International Spread and Management of Conflicts. See also http://www.igcc.ucsd. edu/gleditsch2.php, 2002.

Lemarchand, Rene, 1999, *Ethnicity as Myth: The View from the Central Africa.* Occasional Paper, Centre of African Studies, University of Copenhagen, May.

Lerner D., 1968, *The Passing of Traditional Society: Modernising the Middle Eas.* New York: Free Press.

Lipset S.M., 1959, "Some social requisites of Democracy: Economic development and political legitimacy", *American Political Science Review* 53, 1.

—, 1960, P*olitical man: The Social basis of Politics.* New York: Doubleday.

Metumera, D., 2010, "Democracy and the Challenge of Ethno-Nationalism in Nigeria's Fourth Republic: Interrogating Institutional Mechanisms", *Journal of Peace, Conflict and Development*, Issue 15.

Morrison, D.G. and H.M. Stevenson, 1972, "Cultural Pluralism, Modernisation and conflict: An Empirical Analysis of sources of instability in African Nations", *Canadian Journal of Political Science*. V, 1, March.

Ninsin, Kwame, 2006, "The Contradictions and Ironies of Elections in Africa", *Africa Development* XXXI, 3.

Nnoli, Okwudiba, 1978, *Ethnic Politics in Nigeria.* Enugu: Fourth Dimension Publishers (Revised second edition, 2008).

Nnoli, Okwudiba, 1995, *Ethnicity and Development in Nigeria.* Aldershot: Avebury.

—, 1998, *Ethnic conflicts in Nigeria.* Dakar: CODESRIA.

Nwokedi, Emeka, 1995, *Politics of Democratisation: Changing Authoritarian Regimes in Sub-Saharan Africa.* Hamburg: Alexander Von-Humboldt Foundation.

Nwabueze, B.O., 1993, *Democratisation.* Ibadan: Spectrum Law Publishing.

Nzongola-Ntalaja, Georges (2004), "Citizenship, Political Violence, and Democratization in Africa," *Global Governance* 10.

Nzongola-Ntalaja, Georges, 2001, "The Democracy Project in Africa: The Journey so far", *Nigerian Social Scientist* 1, 1, March.

Obi Cyril, 2001, T*he Changing Forms of Identity Politics in Nigeria under Economic Adjustment: The Case of the Oil Minorities Movement of the Niger Delta.* Uppsala: Nordic Africa Institute.

Okonta, Ike, 2007, "Niger Delta: Behind the Mask: Ijaw Militia Fight the Oil Cartel", in World War 4 Report, http://ww4report.com

Olowu, Dele, Adebayo Williams and Kayode Soremekun (eds), 1999, *Governance and Democratisation in West Africa.* Dakar: CODESRIA.

Omeje, Kenneth, 2005, "Enyimba Enyi: The Comeback of Igbo nationalism in Nigeria", *Review of African Political Economy* 32, 106.

Osaghae, Eghosa, 1995, *Structural Adjustment and Ethnicity in Nigeria.* Research Report No. 98. Uppsala: Nordic Africa Institute.

Otite, Onugu, 1990, *Ethnic Pluralism and Ethnicity in Nigeria.* Ibadan: Shaneson.

Rothchild, Donald, 1986, "Interethnic conflict and Policy Analysis in Africa", *Ethnic and Racial Studies* 9, 1, January.

Salih, M.A. Mohammed and John Markakis, 1998, *Ethnicity and the state in Eastern Africa.* Uppsala: Nordic Africa Institute.

Sancton, T.A., 1987, "Democracy's fragile flower spreads its roots", *Time* 130, 28.

Shehadi, S. Kamal, 1993, *Ethnic Self-determination and the Break-up of States.* IISI ADELPHI Paper 283, December.

Ukiwo, Ukoha, 2007, "From 'Pirates' to 'Militants': A Historical Perspective on Anti-State and Anti-Oil Company Mobilization Among the Ijaw of Warri, Western Niger Delta", *African Affairs* 106: 425.

Vanhanen, Tatu, 1997, *Prospects of Democratisation: A study of 172 countries.* New York: Routledge.

Yere, Michel, 2007, "Reconfiguring Nationhood in Côte d'Ivoire?" in Obi, Cyril, *Perspectives on Côte d'Ivoire: Between Political Breakdown and Post-Conflict Peace.* Discussion Paper 39.Uppsala: Nordic Africa Institute.

DISCUSSION PAPERS PUBLISHED BY THE INSTITUTE

Recent issues in the series are available electronically for download free of charge
www.nai.uu.se

1. Kenneth Hermele and Bertil Odén, *Sanctions and Dilemmas. Some Implications of Economic Sanctions against South Africa.* 1988. 43 pp. ISBN 91-7106-286-6

2. Elling Njål Tjönneland, *Pax Pretoriana. The Fall of Apartheid and the Politics of Regional Destabilisation.* 1989. 31 pp. ISBN 91-7106-292-0

3. Hans Gustafsson, Bertil Odén and Andreas Tegen, *South African Minerals. An Analysis of Western Dependence.* 1990. 47 pp. ISBN 91-7106-307-2

4. Bertil Egerö, *South African Bantustans. From Dumping Grounds to Battlefronts.* 1991. 46 pp. ISBN 91-7106-315-3

5. Carlos Lopes, *Enough is Enough! For an Alternative Diagnosis of the African Crisis.* 1994. 38 pp. ISBN 91-7106-347-1

6. Annika Dahlberg, *Contesting Views and Changing Paradigms.* 1994. 59 pp. ISBN 91-7106-357-9

7. Bertil Odén, *Southern African Futures. Critical Factors for Regional Development in Southern Africa.* 1996. 35 pp. ISBN 91-7106-392-7

8. Colin Leys and Mahmood Mamdani, *Crisis and Reconstruction – African Perspectives.* 1997. 26 pp. ISBN 91-7106-417-6

9. Gudrun Dahl, *Responsibility and Partnership in Swedish Aid Discourse.* 2001. 30 pp. ISBN 91-7106-473-7

10. Henning Melber and Christopher Saunders, *Transition in Southern Africa – Comparative Aspects.* 2001. 28 pp. ISBN 91-7106-480-X

11. *Regionalism and Regional Integration in Africa.* 2001. 74 pp. ISBN 91-7106-484-2

12. Souleymane Bachir Diagne, et al., *Identity and Beyond: Rethinking Africanity.* 2001. 33 pp. ISBN 91-7106-487-7

13. Georges Nzongola-Ntalaja, et al., *Africa in the New Millennium.* Edited by Raymond Suttner. 2001. 53 pp. ISBN 91-7106-488-5

14. *Zimbabwe's Presidential Elections 2002.* Edited by Henning Melber. 2002. 88 pp. ISBN 91-7106-490-7

15. Birgit Brock-Utne, *Language, Education and Democracy in Africa.* 2002. 47 pp. ISBN 91-7106-491-5

16. Henning Melber et al., *The New Partnership for Africa's development (NEPAD).* 2002. 36 pp. ISBN 91-7106-492-3

17. Juma Okuku, *Ethnicity, State Power and the Democratisation Process in Uganda.* 2002. 42 pp. ISBN 91-7106-493-1

18. Yul Derek Davids, et al., *Measuring Democracy and Human Rights in Southern Africa.* Compiled by Henning Melber. 2002. 50 pp. ISBN 91-7106-497-4

19. Michael Neocosmos, Raymond Suttner and Ian Taylor, *Political Cultures in Democratic South Africa.* Compiled by Henning Melber. 2002. 52 pp. ISBN 91-7106-498-2

20. Martin Legassick, *Armed Struggle and Democracy. The Case of South Africa.* 2002. 53 pp. ISBN 91-7106-504-0

21. Reinhart Kössler, Henning Melber and Per Strand, *Development from Below. A Namibian Case Study.* 2003. 32 pp. ISBN 91-7106-507-5

22. Fred Hendricks, *Fault-Lines in South African Democracy. Continuing Crises of Inequality and Injustice.* 2003. 32 pp. ISBN 91-7106-508-3

23. Kenneth Good, *Bushmen and Diamonds. (Un) Civil Society in Botswana.* 2003. 39 pp. ISBN 91-7106-520-2

24. Robert Kappel, Andreas Mehler, Henning Melber and Anders Danielson, *Structural Stability in an African Context.* 2003. 55 pp. ISBN 91-7106-521-0

25. Patrick Bond, *South Africa and Global Apartheid. Continental and International Policies and Politics.* 2004. 45 pp. ISBN 91-7106-523-7

26. Bonnie Campbell (ed.), *Regulating Mining in Africa. For whose benefit?* 2004. 89 pp. ISBN 91-7106-527-X

27. Suzanne Dansereau and Mario Zamponi, *Zimbabwe – The Political Economy of Decline.* Compiled by Henning Melber. 2005. 43 pp. ISBN 91-7106-541-5

28. Lars Buur and Helene Maria Kyed, *State Recognition of Traditional Authority in Mozambique. The nexus of Community Representation and State Assistance.* 2005. 30 pp. ISBN 91-7106-547-4

29. Hans Eriksson and Björn Hagströmer, *Chad – Towards Democratisation or Petro-Dictatorship?* 2005. 82 pp.ISBN 91-7106-549-

30. Mai Palmberg and Ranka Primorac (eds), *Skinning the Skunk – Facing Zimbabwean Futures.* 2005. 40 pp. ISBN 91-7106-552-0

31. Michael Brüntrup, Henning Melber and Ian Taylor, *Africa, Regional Cooperation and the World Market – Socio-Economic Strategies in Times of Global Trade Regimes.* Com-piled by Henning Melber. 2006. 70 pp. ISBN 91-7106-559-8

32. Fibian Kavulani Lukalo, *Extended Handshake or Wrestling Match? – Youth and Urban Culture Celebrating Politics in Kenya.* 2006.58 pp. ISBN 91-7106-567-9

33. Tekeste Negash, *Education in Ethiopia: From Crisis to the Brink of Collapse.* 2006. 55 pp. ISBN 91-7106-576-8

34. Fredrik Söderbaum and Ian Taylor (eds) *Micro-Regionalism in West Africa. Evidence from Two Case Studies.* 2006. 32 pp. ISBN 91-7106-584-9

35. Henning Melber (ed.), *On Africa – Scholars and African Studies.* 2006. 68 pp. ISBN 978-91-7106-585-8

36. Amadu Sesay, *Does One Size Fit All? The Sierra Leone Truth and Reconciliation Commission Revisited.* 2007. 56 pp. ISBN 978-91-7106-586-5

37. Karolina Hulterström, Amin Y. Kamete and Henning Melber, *Political Opposition in African Countries – The Case of Kenya, Namibia, Zambia and Zimbabwe.* 2007. 86 pp. ISBN 978-7106-587-2

38. Henning Melber (ed.), *Governance and State Delivery in Southern Africa. Examples from Botswana, Namibia and Zimbabwe.* 2007. 65 pp. ISBN 978-91-7106-587-2

39. Cyril Obi (ed.), *Perspectives on Côte d'Ivoire: Between Political Breakdown and Post-Conflict Peace.* 2007. 66 pp. ISBN 978-91-7106-606-6

40. Anna Chitando, *Imagining a Peaceful Society. A Vision of Children's Literature in a Post-Conflict Zimbabwe.* 2008. 26 pp. ISBN 978-91-7106-623-7

41. Olawale Ismail, *The Dynamics of Post-Conflict Reconstruction and Peace Building in West Africa. Between Change and Stability.* 2009.52 pp. ISBN 978-91-7106-637-4

42. Ron Sandrey and Hannah Edinger, *Examining the South Africa–China Agricultural Relationship.* 2009. 58 pp. ISBN 978-91-7106-643-5

43. Xuan Gao, *The Proliferation of Anti-Dumping and Poor Governance in Emerging Economies.* 2009. 41 pp. ISBN 978-91-7106-644-2

44. Lawal Mohammed Marafa, *Africa's Business and Development Relationship with China. Seeking Moral and Capital Values of the Last Economic Frontier.* 2009. xx pp. ISBN 978-91-7106-645-9

45. Mwangi wa Githinji, *Is That a Dragon or an Elephant on Your Ladder? The Potential Impact of China and India on Export Led Growth in African Countries.* 2009. 40 pp. ISBN 978-91-7106-646-6

46. Jo-Ansie van Wyk, *Cadres, Capitalists, Elites and Coalitions. The ANC, Business and Development in South Africa.* 2009. 61 pp. ISBN 978-91-7106-656-5

47. Elias Courson, *Movement for the Emancipation of the Niger Delta (MEND). Political Marginalization, Repression and Petro-Insurgency in the Niger Delta.*2009. 30 pp. ISBN 978-91-7106-657-2

48. Babatunde Ahonsi, *Gender Violence and HIV/AIDS in Post-Conflict West Africa. Issues and Responses.* 2010. 38 pp. ISBN 978-91-7106-665-7

49. Usman Tar and Abba Gana Shettima, *Endangered Democracy? The Struggle over Secularism and its Implications for Politics and Democracy in Nigeria.* 2010. 21 pp. ISBN 978-91-7106-666-4

50. Garth Andrew Myers, *Seven Themes in African Urban Dynamics.*2010. 28 pp. ISBN 978-91-7106-677-0

51. Abdoumaliq Simone, *The Social Infrastructures of City Life in Contemporary Africa.* 2010. 33 pp. ISBN 978-91-7106-678-7

52. Li Anshan, *Chinese Medical Cooperation in Africa. With Special Emphasis on the Medical Teams and Anti-Malaria Campaign.* 2011. 24 pp. ISBN 978-91-7106-683-1

53. Folashade Hunsu, *Zangbeto: Navigating the Spaces Between Oral art, Communal Security And Conflict Mediation in Badagry, Nigeria.* 2011. 27 pp. ISBN 978-91-7106-688-6

54. Jeremiah O. Arowosegbe, *Reflections on the Challenge of Reconstructing Post-Conflict States in West Africa: Insights from Claude Ake's Political Writings.*
2011. 40 pp. ISBN 978-91-7106-689-3

55. Bertil Odén, *The Africa Policies of Nordic Countries and the Erosion of the Nordic Aid Model: A comparative study.*
2011. 66 pp. ISBN 978-91-7106-691-6

56. Angela Meyer, *Peace and Security Cooperation in Central Africa: Developments, Challenges and Prospects.*
2011. 47 pp ISBN 978-91-7106-693-0

57. Godwin R. Murunga, *Spontaneous or Premeditated? Post-Election Violence in Kenya.*
2011. 58 pp. ISBN 978-91-7106-694-7

58. David Sebudubudu & Patrick Molutsi, *The Elite as a Critical Factor in National Development: The Case of Botswana.*
2011. 48 pp. ISBN 978-91-7106-695-4

59. Sabelo J. Ndlovu-Gatsheni, *The Zimbabwean Nation-State Project. A Historical Diagnosis of Identity and Power-Based Conflicts in a Postcolonial State.*
2011. 97 pp. ISBN 978-91-7106-696-1

60. Jide Okeke, *Why Humanitarian Aid in Darfur is not a Practice of the 'Responsibility to Protect'.*
2011. 45 pp. ISBN 978-91-7106-697-8

61. Florence Odora Adong, *Recovery and Development Politics. Options for Sustainable Peacebuilding in Northern Uganda.*
2011, 72 pp. ISBN 978-91-7106-698-5

62. Osita A. Agbu, *Ethnicity and Democratisation in Africa. Challenges for Politics and Development.*
2011, 30 pp. ISBN 978-91-7106-699-2

www.ingramcontent.com/pod-product-compliance
Lightning Source LLC
Chambersburg PA
CBHW080210300326
41934CB00039B/3445